The Healing POWER of Love

TWENTY-THIRD PUBLICATIONS
185 WILLOW STREET • PO BOX 180 • MYSTIC, CT 06355
TEL: 1-800-321-0411 • FAX: 1-800-572-0788
E-MAIL: ttpubs@aol.com • www.twentythirdpublications.com

NOVALIS

Novalis
49 Front Street East, 2nd Floor
Toronto, Ontario, Canada
M5E 1B3
Phone: 1-800-387-7164 or (416) 363-3303
Fax: 1-800-204-4140 or (416) 363-9409
Email: novalis@interlog.com
ISBN: 2-89507-526-3

Twenty-Third Publications
A Division of Bayard
185 Willow Street
P.O. Box 180
Mystic, CT 06355
(860) 536-2611 or (800) 321-0411
www.twentythirdpublications.com
ISBN:1-58595-363-6

Library of Congress Catalog Card Number: 2004107165
Printed in the U.S.A.

Contents

The real battle our world is fighting—and losing on so many fronts—is against loneliness and the lack of love. Unless we face this crisis head-on and identify it as the root cause of most of our problems, the vast resources we expend on treating its myriad symptoms—alcohol, drugs, overeating, excessive shopping, over-intellectualizing, indulging, rape, violence—will be wasted.

The problem is greater than the symptoms. The problem is loneliness, isolation, bitterness, anxiety, and despair. That is why it is not a question of how many pills we take, or how many electronic messages we transmit, or how many police

1

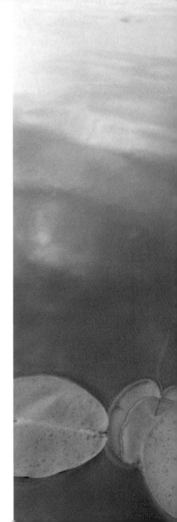

> **The fundamental problem of life is the problem of love.**
>
>

officers we put on the streets, or how many laws we enact; if love is not there, nothing is going to heal the real illness from which we are suffering.

Advances in science and technology may certainly help, but they are not the answer, because they don't deal with the root cause of the problem. They deal only with the symptoms. And the result? More loneliness, more headaches, more boredom, more drugs, more intoxication, more fear, more killing, more prisons, more divorces, more sadness, more pain, more apathy, more psychotherapists, more stupidity, more tears, more death. Who wants to live like this?

It is through our basic relationships with God and others that we find the meaning of life and reach the fulfillment that God intends for us.

The fundamental problem of life is the problem of love. Without real love nothing else seems to make sense or to matter. We have a fundamental need to be loved, lovable, and loving. No fulfillment is possible without love. Love has the power to heal us, to renew us, to make us safe, to bring us deep joy, and to bring us closer to God and to each other. To think that we can exist apart from others and from the universe is an illusion. Love redefines our very existence in relationship to others, and brings about heaven on Earth.

One day we will realize that the things that cannot be counted or measured mean more in life than the things that can be counted. Why? Because they are the most real and the most valuable. This is what Antoine de Saint Exupéry (1900-1944), the author of *The Little Prince*, meant when he wrote: "It is only with the heart that one can see rightly. What is essential is invisible to the eye."

And when St. Paul was talking about faith, hope, and love, he indicated clearly which was preeminent: "...the greatest of these is love" (1 Cor 13:13). In that same epistle, he also wrote:

> If I speak in the tongues of mortals and angels, but do not have love, I am a noisy gong or a clanging cymbal. And if I have prophetic powers, and understand all mysteries and all knowledge, and if I have all faith, so as to remove mountains, but do not have love, I am nothing. If I give away all my possessions, and if I hand over my body so that I may boast, but do not have love, I gain nothing (1 Cor 13:1–3).

Love is, indeed, the greatest power known to humankind. This tells us that, at the end of the day and of life, what we human beings really want is something that surpasses the desires for recognition, power, money, and things. What we really want is love. Love can heal and transform our lives. If we go to the ends of the earth and of ourselves to find this love, we will be rewarded with an understanding of the very reason we are here.

In this little book, which is part of the *Healing Power* series, I hope to shed new light on the love that helps heal us by bringing us a little closer to home. Please keep in mind while reading this book the line written about 400 years ago by John of the Cross: "When there is no love put love and there you will find love."

Bon voyage through these pages, which are my gift to you, a gift that you richly deserve. Love be with you in every word you read and with every step you take on this journey.

CHAPTER ONE

What Does Love Mean?

Little children, let us love, not in word or speech, but in truth and action. And by this we will know that we are from the truth and will reassure our hearts before him whenever our hearts condemn us; for God is greater than our hearts, and he knows everything.

      ☐ 1 JOHN 3:18–20

Throughout our lives, we all experience religious, ethnic, cultural, psychological, and political differences that separate us from one another. But there is also common ground that connects us.

The way we relate to others, to the world, and to God defines who and what we really are. Not to relate to anyone or to anything is not an option. We are born helpless, utterly dependent on others.

Therefore, to relate or not to relate to others cannot be the question. The question is only *how* do we relate to others? When we inquire of another, "How are you?" we imply, perhaps unwittingly, questions like, "How are you relating to your family, friends, things, and situations?" To even think that one has nothing to do with others is an illusion. All human beings respond to love when they know they are loved. This is precisely what makes them feel good.

Openness is part of the definition of being human. We are relational. "No man is an island" is a familiar axiom. A person cannot survive alone. We coexist on the most basic biological and physical levels. We also coexist on the level of thoughts, emotions, and souls. "We are, each of us," best-selling author John Powell, S.J., says, "the product of those who have loved us…or refused to love us."

The same can be said when it comes to groups and even nations. We can enrich as well as destroy one another, if we so choose. We are, like it or not, inter-dependent. We are responsible for each other. The

Second Vatican Council was explicit on this point, especially in *Gaudium et Spes:*

> In every group or nation, there is an ever-increasing number of men and women who are conscious that they themselves are the artisans and the authors of the culture of their community. Throughout the world there is a similar growth in the combined sense of independence and responsibility. Such a development is of paramount importance for the spiritual and moral maturity of the human race. This truth grows clearer if we consider how the world is becoming unified and how we have the duty to build a better world based upon truth and justice. Thus we are witnesses of the birth of a new humanism, one in which man is defined first of all by his responsibility toward his brothers and toward history (55).

We are relational. We are what we love. But what is this thing called love?

In this present age we use the word "love" casually and indiscriminately to describe anything we like or take great pleasure in; e.g., "I love chocolate," "I love dogs," "I love my car," "I love to watch TV," and so on.

Indeed, this casual usage has become so common-place and pervasive that one can lose sight of the fact that love is the greatest force in the world. Perhaps this offhand use tells us how starved we are for the real thing.

So what is love, and how do we find it?

The Many Faces of Love

Love can take different forms and shapes. Let's quick-ly review some of them.

Parent/child love (entire family included) between a father, a mother, and a child is the euphoric love of protection, security, and satisfaction. Psychiatrist Erich Fromm (1900-1980), in his book *The Art of Loving*, described this kind of love by saying: "Infantile love follows the principle: 'I love because I am loved.' Mature love follows the principle: 'I am loved because I love.' Immature love says: 'I love you because I need you.' Mature love says: 'I need you because I love you.'" What Fromm is saying about infantile and immature love applies to the love of cer-tain adults who psychologically and spiritually did not grow up.

Brotherly love (love of friends included) is the kind of love that includes all human beings. This is where our "neighbor" of the Bible becomes our "brother" or "sister." Brotherly love indicates that we are all one and that we belong to the family of humankind.

Love can take different forms and shapes.

Erotic love is the type of love that strives for complete union with another person. Erotic love is, by its very nature, exclusive. It can be uniquely fulfilling when it conveys the very essence of being to the other, and it can be deceptive and short-lived when it is based on superficial attractions or on fantasy.

Emotional love can be mistakenly identified with a certain feeling. Although often accompanied by powerful emotions, love is not essentially just an emotion or a feeling. It is a choice. True love does not reduce the other to an "it"—an object of consumption. True love relates to a "thou." People who considered Marilyn Monroe extremely attractive and made her a sex goddess related to her at the level of the emotional feeling she inspired in them. Her real personality was completely concealed. Some of her biographers have suggested that the reason she took her life was that she didn't feel that anyone was really interested in her as a unique person. People were after a glamour girl, movie star, or sex object. How absurd life can be if true love is missing! Love is not a mere feeling. Love is a choice, an act of will, a determination, and a power—the power to accomplish anything.

Love of God is the religious type of love. God's love for each of us is unconditional, unmerited, and unsolicited. Our appropriate answer is meant to be a resounding yes to accept, and live by, this love. St. John says: "God is love, and those who abide in love, abide in God, and God abides in them" (1 Jn 4:16).

Another Way to Look at Love

Another way of looking at love can be summarized as follows:

Immature love consists in asking. A child simply asks. "Give me this, give me that," implies: "If you don't give me what I am asking for, then you don't love me." This attitude is not necessarily wrong for a child. But it is inappropriate for adults to remain stuck in this kind of infantilism.

Generous love consists in the act of giving. Giving is good. But one can be stuck there, too. Do-gooders may want to give money, time, and effort without receiving anything in return, but often this is because if they accept anything, their egos would be hurt. These are very generous people, but their generosity is built around the ego part of their personalities; they want to project a righteous image of themselves.

Mature love consists in giving and receiving. Giving and receiving flow like breathing in and breathing out. You give something and you receive something else. The one who receives likes to feel that he or she is able to give back something; maybe a smile, maybe a gesture of gratitude, maybe a lesson in human relationship.

Unconditional love consists in being love. You forget giving and taking. You identify with the whole. You identify with God, who is pure love. "I am the way," said Jesus (Jn 14:6). Christ cannot do anything but love. Love is the way. A loving person simply loves. Love becomes a natural function. You love unconditionally. You love because it is in your nature to love. No one asks the flower to fill the field with beauty and fragrance. It just does. Likewise, love transforms the world.

Still Another Way to Look at Love

There is another way, probably the best-known, to look at love. It uses the three Greek words, *eros, phileo, agape,* that are rendered by the one English word "love."

Eros (originally, the god of love in Greek mythology) usually suggests sensual desire. Sometimes it is confused with lust or sexuality. In fact, it is much more comprehensive and complicated.

Eros is not a mere expression of libido. It also can be a sublimated libido, in which case it is the drive of life. Eros drives us toward someone or something that can fill a void in the very core of our being and without which we are at a loss. Eros demands an instant satisfaction. Profound frustration will follow if satisfaction is delayed or even if, as often happens, satisfaction occurs and we keep looking for still further satisfaction.

We also can feel burned out when what satisfied us for some reason suddenly leaves us empty because that reason no longer exists. This is especially true when covenants and hearts are broken and the so-called love becomes the root of irritability. Since eros arises from human needs for personal growth and human communion through sex, family, and friendship, it dies when this or that need is satisfied. That is why one cannot live a truly fulfilled and happy life by eros alone.

For Sigmund Freud (1865-1939), eros is the power that "holds together everything in the world." Carl Jung (1875-1961) agreed with Freud on this, but he went further, seeing in eros an innate drive toward the sacred. In this sense the sexual union of marriage conveys an authentic experience of the divine. Marriage is a sacrament that conveys special graces to the entire family. Like Freud and Jung, theologian Paul Tillich (1886-1965) considered eros as a special unitive power, and he postulated that our love for God can be eros, because it is the drive that unites us with the source of our being.

Moreover, eros can be taken to include the thirst and longing frequently expressed in the Bible and by the mystics throughout the centuries. Perhaps we can call this eros a heavenly eros if it is not detached from the earthly eros of Genesis 1—3 and the Song of Songs. The thirst for God is particularly remarkable in the book of Psalms. For example:

As a deer longs for flowing streams,
so my soul longs for you, O God.
My soul thirsts for God, for the living God.
When shall I come and behold the face of God?
(Ps 42:1–2)

O God, you are my God,
I seek you, my soul thirsts for you;
my flesh faints for you,
as in a dry and weary land where there is no water.
(Ps 63:1)

Augustine wrote in his *Confessions* of the restlessness of the human heart: "Our hearts are restless until they can find peace in you." Gregory the Great was sometimes called the "doctor of desire." St. Bernard used the allegorical interpretation of the Song of Songs to explain certain aspects of the spiritual life. Teresa of Avila and John of the Cross used erotic imagery to describe the profound union between the soul and God. For example, John wrote:

Where have You hidden,
Beloved, and left me moaning?
You fled like the stag
After wounding me;
I went out calling You, and You were gone.

Why, since You wounded
This heart, don't You heal it?
And why, since You stole it from me,
Do you leave it so,
And fail to carry off what You have stolen?

Extinguish these miseries,
Since no one else can stamp them out;
And may my eyes behold You,
Because you are their light,
And I would open them to You alone.

Show me your presence
That I may die at the sight of your beauty,
Since the pain of love can only be healed
By the presence and sight of the beloved.
Withdraw them, Beloved,
I am taking flight!

In this sense, eros is not only the longing to be united with God—the supremely beautiful, true, and good—but also the drive for transformation and completion. It is a constructive energy that infuses our search for God, as it moves things toward their goal. Human achievements in art, science, and culture can be related to this energy, too, for it is the stimulus behind personal growth and the rise of civilizations and the building of cities. Eros, however, can be misunderstood, misdefined, and misused; by itself, it is not sufficient for a healthy life.

Phileo is the love of family members and friends. It is the love of others because they are worthy of love. It is the deep camaraderie and friendship that seeks to give and take; and, above all, it desires the other person's well-being. It is generally described as rational, peaceful, and stable. If we don't have this kind of love we are in trouble. Isolation, restlessness, unhappiness, resentment, anger, and depression are the result of the absence of this love. In many cases, these troubles are often manifested as physical illnesses such as headaches, stomach aches, heart disease, and cancer, to name just a few.

Agape is God's love. This kind of supernatural love is the purest, deepest, and truest kind of love. It is revealed to us supremely through the Son of God: "For God so loved the world that he gave his only Son, so that everyone who believes in him may not perish but may have eternal life" (Jn 3:16). God wants to generate in us, and through us in others, this kind of love.

Such a love is not based on the worthiness of the object of love but on the very character of the person loving. Here we love others not because of, but in spite of. Here emotions play a secondary role. Our will, with God's grace, is given the primary role. Love is the execution of a commandment. C.S. Lewis (1898-1963) wrote in *The Four Loves*: "Eros, honored without reservation and obeyed unconditionally, becomes demon…. He cannot of himself be what, nevertheless, he must be if he is to remain Eros. He needs help; therefore needs to be ruled. The god dies or becomes a demon unless he obeys God."

Jesus gave to his disciples—and through them to us and to all believers—a new commandment: "I give you a new commandment, that you love one another. Just I have loved you, you also should love one another. By this everyone will know that you are my disciples, if you have love for one another" (Jn 13:34–35). This is the kind of love that he demonstrated when he died on the cross for our salvation.

> "I give you a new commandment, that you love one another."

It is this same divine, supernatural, unconditional, unchangeable, unlimited, and everlasting love that he wants us to have in our hearts, no matter what the circumstances are, even if the other happens to be the enemy. "Love your enemies" (Mt 5:44), he commanded. We need not understand how we can do it. We need only to understand that God's love is the very power that moves us in that direction, without demanding or expecting any return from the neighbor we love.

Agape is a divine and supernatural power flowing from the Father to the Son, and through him to the disciples, to us, and to the world. It is agape that guides eros along the true path and enables it to be integrated in the sacred realm. Without agape, eros may remain alienated from the focus of Jesus Christ that is a higher calling "for the sake of the kingdom of heaven" (Mt 19:12).

In a mystical experience, a transformed and trans-figured eros is often present side by side with agape. The love of God does not abolish anything in the human psyche. It works within the framework of human life as God has created and perfects it. Its extraordinary power enables us before it obligates us. Eros may lead to broken covenants. Agape effects continuous revival, resurrection, and endurance.

Perhaps, then, we should speak of "erotic agape" or "agapistic eros"—a marriage between eros and agape—to signal that eros and agape are not always fated to be in conflict, that true love is not just a beautiful concept and an intellectual exercise but an embodied love as well, and that they are united in God. God is the source of our love. God is the true relationship. "God is love" (1 Jn 4:16).

When we talk about different categories of love and classify them under the love of a parent and a child, a love between friends, a love between lovers, and a love for humanity, we do this to highlight certain aspects and nuances of love. But the love that is real and genuine is God's love, and it should lie at the heart of all true relationships.

God's love is universal, and it does not change according to circumstances. The very desire for love proves the existence of God. The other becomes the door to God. We have a compelling urge to be one with the whole and a deep longing to return to the source. An immense love filled with the presence of God is felt—a love that is beyond anything sensible or intellectual because it is coming from the depths of the very soul. It is so whole and total that it makes us shout, "How is it possible to love so much?" or exclaim with Jane Frances de Chantal (1572-1641), "Our love has no name in any language." Likewise, the early Christians understood that agape meant both the love of God and the love of the least of brethren. "By this everyone will know that you are my disciples, if you have love for one another" (Jn 13:35).

In any event, this kind of divine love cannot be the result of our own efforts. We could never love others the way God loves each and every one of us. Only God provides us with this unconditional and unlimited love. It is the very reason for our existence and the key to our true identity. Thomas Merton (1915-1968) wrote: "To say that I am made in the image of God is to say that love is the reason for my existence, for God is love. Love is my true identity. Selflessness is my true self. Love is my true character. Love is my name."

Love is what one is, much more than what one does or says.

FOR YOUR REFLECTION AND RESPONSE

1. The following statements should help you to have a better knowledge of yourself. Check the conclusions that apply to you. I would have felt much better in my life if:

- I had more money
- I was more helpful to others
- I had a bigger house
- I had better communication skills
- I had a Ph.D.
- I was a good listener
- I was more productive
- I had a meaningful goal
- I was always right
- I was happier
- I was promoted at work
- I was more accepted by others
- I was more accepting of others

- I was less burdened with family
- I had more extended family
- Everyone agreed with me
- I was more ready to listen, read, and learn

Then try to name what influences your vision of life. Ask yourself this question, "If I had a short time to live, what would I do first, second, third?"

2. Have you ever felt a visible or invisible support when you were in need of a loving presence? Do you rely on the inner voice that comes from your heart and soul? Did you ever pray for yourself or someone else and have your prayer answered? In the midst of a crisis, have you encountered someone who unexpectedly helped you?

3. Is love the beginning or the end of a journey? Can love be the journey itself? Is love an emotion or a decision, or both, or neither? Does love come and go, or is it a constant way of living? Is the love of your neighbor different from the love of God? How do you define yourself if you are not in a relationship with others? What are some of the most important relationships in your life? Can you change them? Can they change you?

4. When others do not conform their perspective to yours, do you consider them misguided, entitled to their own opinion, or helpful? What is your main obstacle to openness to others? Does forgiveness seem easier when you see others' true motivations and understand where they are coming from? Have you ever seen in your enemies the shadow of what you don't like in yourself? In order to grasp the depth of the real you, what would you like to share with others, and what would you allow them to share with you?

5. Why do you love your family and friends? Is this because you need them? Why do you love a stranger? Does love need a reason to be love? Is love rational? Can love be just the irrational wisdom of the heart? Why is God called love? Do you see any correlation between love, happiness, and holiness? Do you feel any need for others? When people say, "He or she has a perfect life," what do they mean? Do you think that who and what you love determine who you are?

AFFIRMATION

Repeat this several times a day.

God's love makes me loving and lovable.

PRAYER

Dear God, I have much of everything. I have money, a house, family and friends, prestige, and knowledge. I am full—but I feel empty. I am exuberant and I possess the desire to conquer the world. But I long for the "only one thing" (Lk 10:42) that is necessary.

I thought I was doing everything right. But you said that love is still more important.

The wind of your Spirit is moving within me. A mighty whirlwind is spinning, carrying my false self out the window—away, away, away. My old richness and righteousness are gone. Your love has set me free. Your love has healed me.

Your love is my love. Amen!

CHAPTER TWO

The Ultimate Love Story

"For God so loved the world that he gave his only Son, so that everyone who believes in him may not perish but may have eternal life."

□ JOHN 3:16

If relationships are what life is all about, life is all about love.

Every love story should begin and end with the ultimate love story of all—the story of God and the man and woman who were created in God's image.

It really is all about this greatest relationship that ever was.

God's story is the story of the divine yearning for us and the longing to bring us back to the divine company from the one who had taken us captive. It is the story of the greatest love there is: "For God so loved the world that he gave his only Son, so that everyone who believes in him may not perish but may have eternal life" (Jn 3:16).

There is nothing greater than this love, a love that is a spiritual marriage in which love is stronger than death.

Spiritual Marriage

In the Bible, marriage is a richly symbolic relationship. In the Old Testament, God not only desires to have a marriage with Israel, but is declared the husband of Israel. In the book of Hosea, for example, the Israelites' unfaithfulness to the covenant God made with them is compared to the unfaithfulness of Hosea's wife to their marriage. In both cases adultery has been committed, one spiritual, the other physical. But despite this infidelity, God continued to love the Israelites and Hosea to love his wife.

The Song of Solomon develops this imagery further. This book, so full of symbolism, shows the richness of the love that exists between husband (lover) and wife (his beloved). It also describes both the joy and the pain that characterize all intimate relationships, wedded love being the richest human relationship of all. This extended poem on love and marriage was interpreted allegorically throughout the centuries. Some interpreters saw in this poem a love song between God and Israel. Others thought that it was an allegory pointing to the love relationship between Christ and the Church (his bride).

In the New Testament, rebirth in Jesus Christ gives us a new nature that allows us to have a divine union with him. When Paul wrote, "Anyone united to the Lord becomes one spirit with him" (1 Cor 6:17), he was pointing a union deeper than the physical union of a husband and wife. This union with Christ is so deep that we become "members of his body" (Eph 5:30). This means that, as true believers, we are not only one spirit with him, but also his flesh and bones on Earth. We are the branches of the vine (see Jn 15:5) whose life is flowing through us. Moreover, God is faithful forever (see 1 Cor 1:9). He will not divorce us (see 1 Cor 7:11), and Christ intercedes for us with the Father (see Heb 7:25).

However, this spiritual marriage with the Lord can be broken. God will never break his promises; he will never leave us (see Heb 13:5), and he will unite with us just as a husband unites with his wife and the two become one flesh (see Mt 19:5–6). But we can decide to leave God. He will not force us to stay with him. He does not twist arms. He allows us to go.

God is faithful forever.

But, as the parable of the prodigal son says, "…while he [the prodigal son] was still far off, his father saw him and was filled with compassion; he ran and put his arms around him and kissed him" (Lk 15:20).

This kind of extraordinary love, which surpasses our human understanding, transcends history and geography. Indeed, it is a love that transcended the ancient empires of the Egyptians, the Assyrians, the Greeks and Romans, the Mongols, the Ottomans. Nor can any modern military, political, technological, or cultural superpower ever match the power of the man that the haughty Roman empire allowed to be crucified two thousand years ago, and whose only weapon was love—the love that still changes lives radically. That is why Paul was so adamant in describing this force as "the greatest."

How short-sighted was Napoleon when he said, "God is on the side of the biggest battalions." Indeed, one might say that Napoleon, Alexander the Great, Sennach'erib, and all the prominent figures in the pantheon of secular history are eclipsed by Jesus of Nazareth, who taught us the true meaning of love. True greatness consists not in subjugating people, but in loving them more deeply. We ought to try it earnestly, seriously, and passionately.

"The Greatest of These Is Love"

Speaking about faith, hope, and love, Paul concluded that love is the greatest. In chapter 13 of his first letter to the Corinthians, Paul wrote probably the most inspiring lines ever written on love; they deserve to be taken as guidelines for the understanding of what true love is all about. This is what he writes:

> If I speak in the tongues of mortals and of angels, but do not have love, I am a noisy gong or a clanging cymbal. And if I have prophetic powers, and understand all mysteries and all knowledge, and if I have all faith, so as to remove mountains, but do not have love, I am nothing. If I give away all my possessions, and if I hand over my body so that I may boast, but do not have love, I gain nothing (1 Cor 13:1–3).

Every time I read this passage, I enter a meditative mood of self-scrutiny and examine my deepest motives. I hope you feel much better than I do when you read this chapter.

I invite you to think about what Paul was saying in everyday contemporary terms. We think we are doing the right thing. We work hard at our job to support our family. Great! We keep the house clean, we cook, and we care for the children. Great! We go to church every Sunday, we sing in the choir, we teach the catechism, and we talk to prospective members of our community. Great! We keep the commandments, we know the law, we speak several languages, and we know how to comport ourselves in polite society. Great! We use our skills for the service of the Church. Great! We make generous contributions to build churches and hospitals. Great! We preach the Good News, and we give to the poor. Great!

But—imagine this!—we are "nothing," wrote St. Paul, if "we do not have love." *Nothing*—what a startling word for us who did all these good things! "Nothing" is the opposite of "something." We want to be important and respected in the community, but we are nobodies, nothing, of no account, of no value. We can make detailed lists of our splendid achievements and services for others and even for the Lord, but if we don't have love, all the things we have done are nothing. *We* are nothing. When love is not there, nothing counts. If we miss love, we miss life.

But what is love? Can you think of a comprehensive and precise definition of love? Paul does not define it. He names its qualities and expressions. Maybe this is a better way to do it. How do you define music? You will have a better idea about music if, instead of reading a twenty-five page article about it, you just listen to a beautiful symphony.

Qualities and Expressions of Love

Love is patient. Love waits and waits and waits. It never gives up. In every life, there are valleys—setbacks, disappointments, sorrows, losses, illnesses, difficulties of all kinds with our own families, our fellow workers, neighbors, strangers. Francis de Sales recommends having a patience with all the world, but first of all with yourself, because "Patience," as Gregory of the sixth century affirmed, "is the root and guardian of all virtues." It certainly pays to be patient.

Love is kind. Kindness is the sum of those things we do to show our love, such as writing thank-you notes, sending flowers to someone, running errands for an elderly person, dropping off a meal, reading to someone with impaired vision, and similar acts. It is love in action. William Penn (1644-1718) said: "I expect to pass through life but once. If therefore there be any kindness I can show, or any good thing I can do to any fellow-being, let me do it now, and not defer or neglect it, as I shall not pass this way again."

Love is patient. Love is kind.

Kindness is power, not weakness. It takes great power to be truly kind, to embrace the weakness of the weak in order to heal them. For Friedrich Nietzsche (1844-1900), the philosopher who wished for supermen, kindness makes strong people waste their energies on lepers, cripples, and handicapped people. How wrong are all those who think and act along these lines! Kindness has enormous strength. Kindness is a truly revolutionary concept if we think seriously about it. Paul wrote: "God's foolishness is wiser than human wisdom, and God's weakness is stronger than human strength" (1 Cor 1:25).

Love is not envious or boastful or arrogant or rude. Love is not jealous. In most of us there is something of the poison envy, as some people call it, described in the stories of Cain and Abel (see Gen 4:4–8); Sarah and Hagar (see Gen 16:5–6; 21:9–10); Joseph and his brothers (see Gen 37:3–11, 19–20); Saul and David (see 1 Sam 18:8–9, 29); Miriam, Aaron, and Moses (see Num 12:1–14); and of the prodigal son's elder brother (see Lk 15:25–30). This brother, for example, was able to love his younger sibling as long as he was far away. But he was furious to see this disgraced boy completely restored to the arms of his father.

Envy and jealousy arise from possessiveness. Love is not possessive. When one loves, one has the sense of being a member of the family of God and thinks of all members as precious. A loving member is not ill-mannered or rude or arrogant. A loving member listens to others; admits personal flaws or shortcomings, says; "I'm sorry," "I was wrong," or "Please, forgive me"; does not undermine others' authority by taking control of conversations and situations; does not enjoy embarrassing others; and does not have a short temper. Francis de Sales said: "Love is a magistrate who exercises his authority without noise, without policemen or sergeants."

Love is not possessive.

[Love] does not insist on its own way. No selfishness is allowed. Love

always gives and always has something to give. We all have limitations. We should not use these limitations as an excuse for not giving. We can always give what we have. When Peter and John were going to the temple to pray, a crippled beggar approached them asking for alms. Peter said to him: "I have no silver and gold, but what I have I give you; in the name of Jesus Christ of Nazareth, stand up and walk" (Acts 3:6). Acceptance of others frees us from our stubbornness in thinking that there is only one way—my way.

[Love] is not irritable or resentful. To have a temper is not a good quality. To be in control of one's emotions is. When we try to understand others and their real motivations, it is always wiser, if not easier, to take a loving attitude. Maybe they were sick, were feeling a deep sorrow, or were overwhelmed by a series of disappointments. Maybe they were mistreated. Maybe they were misinformed. Likewise, a good self-examination is advisable when one feels vulnerable, irritable, and upset. To understand why other people are upset or why we are upset is very important for the capacity to remain in love. If we are too sensitive and keep account of all the wrongs done against us, we may look for evil when none was intended. In love there is a strength that helps to discern one's heart and feelings.

[Love] does not rejoice in wrongdoing, but rejoices in the truth. Love always looks for the good and the positive instead of the bad and the negative. Love is not blind. Love sees and rejoices in the truth. Love does not rejoice over wrongdoings or errors. Love looks for the truth. Philip Neri is reported to have said to a woman who confessed having spread slanderous reports: "Go into the market, buy a chicken, pluck out its feathers, and throw them away, and return to me." She did. "Now go back and bring all the feathers you have scattered," said Philip. "That is impossible," said the woman. "Yes," said Philip. "Likewise, your words of slander have been carried about in every direction, and you cannot recall them."

Aesop, of fable fame, said, "Nothing is better than tongue. It is the bond of civil society, the organ of truth and reason, the instrument of our praise of God.... [And] the tongue is [also] the worst thing. It is lies, blasphemies, the source of division and war."

[Love] bears all things, believes all things, hopes all things, endures all things. Love never ends. Being good and loving without measure is a reflection of eternity. Novelist John Steinbeck, in his book *East of Eden*, said it well: "We have only one story. All novels, all poetry, are built on the never-ending contest in ourselves of

good and evil. And it occurs to me that evil must constantly respawn, while good, while virtue, is immortal. Vice has always a new fresh young face, while virtue is venerable as nothing else in the world is."

Love sees and rejoices in the truth.

But love—bearing, believing, hoping, enduring all things—is not easy, especially in a culture that seems to reward the adulterer, the criminal, the clever one, the sophisticated thief, the liar; don't we find reasons to justify their actions and sometimes even praise them? It is not easy to love by remaining faithful to one's responsibilities and convictions, when the world makes it much easier to put these aside and follow the crowd. The world falls apart if men and women give up believing in principles and stop loving.

In the fourteenth-century spiritual classic, *Imitation of Christ*, Thomas à Kempis echoed Paul:

Nothing is sweeter than love, nothing stronger, nothing higher, nothing wider, nothing more pleasant, nothing fuller nor better in Heaven and Earth; because Love is born of God, and cannot rest but in God, above all created things....Love is swift, sincere, kindly-affectioned, pleasant and delightsome; brave, patient, faithful, prudent, long-suffering, manly, and never seeking itself. For where a person seeketh himself, there he falleth from Love.

Love is circumspect, humble, and upright; not yielding to softness, or to lightness, nor attending to vain things; it is sober, chaste, firm, quiet, and guarded in all the senses. (*Imitation*, III, 5)

We should also mention that in this life love comes always in an incomplete way. It is never finished. It grows and grows and grows. This is its very nature. The pseudo-love that is based on projections and images of the self or on fantasies will be ephemeral. True love is an instrument of ever-increasing life. Loving people may be forgotten, but the Spirit and the flame survive in the love they leave behind.

Love Is the Actual Form of God

At Christmas we travel miles and miles by car, train, boat, airplane to be with those we love. But all of these miles are nothing in comparison to God's journey to the manger of Bethlehem. The story of God's infinite love is the greatest love story of all. It is the actual form of God. Our love for one another is grounded in God's love for us. No wonder we can die for love. The martyrs and the saints did it thousands of times. No wonder we become lovable precisely because of this love. Augustine said it so well: "By loving me, you made me lovable."

In the image of God we have been created. "God is love" (1 Jn 4:16), and so are we. We were created out of love. We exist out of love. We continue to exist out of love. We would be reduced to nothingness should God withhold his love from us, even for a moment. The name of God's gospel is love. The Incarnation of Jesus Christ was the supreme instance of God's love. "For God so loved the world that he gave his only Son, so that everyone who believes in him may not perish but may have eternal life" (Jn 3:16).

Jesus was God's most perfect form and epiphany. In him the transcendent and immanent are merged, and in him also we should grow up—thinking like him, acting like him, loving like him, and reflecting his God-consciousness. And being transformed by his love, we learn to love God totally, unconditionally, and passionately. When we do that, we live the most direct experience of God. Ideally, the people who see us should see Christ's love, and perceive "the love of Christ that surpasses knowledge" (Eph 3:19). Thus are they empowered to receive all that God has for them.

Love…is the power that heals.

This is the kind of love that is able to heal our soul, mind, heart, and body. The true meaning of total love of God is not to love nothing but God, but to love God and to love all in God. Thomas Aquinas (1226-1274) wrote: "Love of our neighbor is included in the love of God."

When John of the Cross speaks about the Living Flame of Love to mean the Holy Spirit, he makes it clear that the whole Christian experience is a work of love, the work of the indwelling Spirit of love.

The Holy Spirit sustains us by bringing the fullness of God to us, and by helping us to live the fullness of life which is God's life of love. Love—the dynamic life interaction of the Trinity, expressed through creation, redemption, and sustenance—is the power that heals. It uses human love to reach out to others and do what God wants done. The curative powers of this love are known even to medical professionals. Gerald Jampolsky, M.D., for example, writes:

> For me the common denominator in all healing is God. And because God and love are one and the same, the common denominator in healing is love. To heal and to be healed is to walk each

day, each hour, each second with God. It is to recognize that God is our only true relationship. To heal is to recognize every encounter with another person as a holy encounter, seeing only the holiness in that person.

When we love others, we become aware of them in a heightened way. We realize that no one of them is unimportant or uninteresting to God, and that every one of them is the road, not the obstacle, to God's love. We accept them as they really are, not as they might appear. We affirm them. We build them up. We affirm God in them as their ultimate reality, and we expand God's work in them as creator, redeemer, and sustainer. We understand that our love for them for Christ's sake is not different from a participation in Christ's love for them. We confirm what Henri Lacordaire (1802-1861), the famous preacher of Notre Dame de Paris, said in describing this reality: "There are not two loves, one heavenly and the other earthly; it is but one sentiment, with the difference that the one is infinite."

We now realize that our journey together is a journey of healing in which we will feel truly alive and well. We also realize that the reality of God-with-us does not mean that we no longer have problems, but that God enters with us into our confusions, dysfunctions—into all problems we may have. In order to know who we really are and how we can solve our problems, we need to see our story as part of God's story and God's story as part of our story. To any challenge we meet there is an answer: love. And since "God is love" (1 Jn 4:8), God is the answer. God is in me. God is in you. God is also in our very relatedness to one another. Like the Trinity, we exist with one another interdependently. And it is the Trinity that defines our true relationships to one another. We share God's nature when we love.

The way we understand God makes all the difference in the world. If we believe in a God of love, then God will be our trusted ally in healing. But if our God is the God of fear, then we will have a very serious problem with the healing process.

FOR YOUR REFLECTION AND RESPONSE

1. Are you really enjoying your life? Do you try to feel fulfilled by trying to have as many experiences as you can, even if they are without any particular focus or any commitment? Does the question, "Is this all there is?" come often to your mind? Are you fooled by your feelings? Does the way you treat others reflect the way God has loved you and treated you? What do you think you most need?

2. Do you suffer from a secret envy? Do you envy other people's position? success? wealth? physical appearance? talents? gifts? possessions? age? charisma? What are the five adjectives that best describe you? What are the five characteristics you would like to see in those who are in contact with you?

3. What is your understanding of God's love? How do you experience God's love? How much does God's love affect your life? Does God's love influence your emotions, decisions, and the way you meet your daily responsibilities? Does God's love change your attitudes and actions toward others? When do you feel is God most real to you?

4. Do you think that psychology has correct and complete answers to the fundamental questions concerning your life? When you consider the meaning of life, do you think that the real questions and answers are to be found in science or in a spirituality that goes much deeper?

5. Do you believe there is such a thing as unconditional love? How did Jesus express love? How did he describe his relationship with God and with you and me? What effect does his understanding of this relationship have in your consciousness and your very being? In the list of the qualities of love given in 1 Corinthians 13, try to replace the word "love" with your name. Is what you read, at that moment, still true?

6. What would you like your last words to be before you leave earth? When your life on earth is about to end, would you prefer to be surrounded by your diplomas, medals, certificates of achievement, or rather by the people you love and care about? Would God see that your projects were more important than the people in your life? Why is it important to love now?

AFFIRMATION

Repeat this several times a day:

The more I love God, the more I love others as myself.

PRAYER

Lord, you are the God of love. You are my first love, my best love, my perfect and most ultimate love. You are the delight of my mind, the thrill of my heart, and the very being of my soul. You are my deepest joy and my ultimate goal.

Thank you for showing me that my life cannot be run, lived, and fulfilled any other way. Thank you for giving me this immensely beautiful grace of uniting with you in a love relationship. I depend solely on your life within me.

Please God, make me a worthy instrument for conveying your love, when your love wants to flow to others through me. Thank you for the grace of having found the meaning of my life that heals me. Amen.

CHAPTER THREE

Heart Matters

*My child, be attentive to my
words; incline your ears
to my sayings. Do not let them
escape from your sight; keep
them within your heart. For they
are life to those who find them,
and healing to all their flesh.
Keep your heart with vigilance,
for from it flow the springs of life.*

◻ PROVERBS 4:20–23

Heart is our blessing, but it
can also be our curse. In
exploring the depths of the
heart, we find, at its very core,
the divine reality of connection—the love connection—so
essential to human life. But this

great openness to others means, at the same time that the negative and destructive factors of life can also affect the self, which has to let go of its boundaries in order to reach out. A loving presence strengthens our immune system and helps to heal and often cure our misfortunes.

At the deepest level of the heart, the experience of loving takes place; this is a marvelous and mysterious experience. But this is where our vulnerability shows up and can make us afraid to love. C.S. Lewis expressed this eloquently in *The Four Loves* when he wrote :

> To love at all is to be vulnerable. Love anything, and your heart will certainly be wrung and possibly broken. If you want to make sure of keeping it intact, you must give your heart to no one, not even to an animal. Wrap it carefully round with hobbies and little luxuries; avoid all entanglements; lock it up safe in the casket or coffin of your selfishness. But in that casket—safe, dark, motionless, airless—it will change. It will not be broken; it will become unbreakable, impenetrable, irredeemable. The alternative to tragedy, or at least to the risk of tragedy, is damnation. The only place outside Heaven where you can be

perfectly safe from all the dangers and perturbations of love is Hell.

At this same level, we also find our uniqueness, purpose, and true self.

The Core of Being

The heart suggests the various holistic dimensions of the self. It is the center, the core of our being, and the innermost region of our lives. Symbolically, it is the source of our emotions. Metaphorically, it is the capacity for intimacy, union, communion, and passion. It is also where the deepest and fullest knowing takes place. Don't we know best with and in our heart? This is because, in the heart's knowing, our intellectual truth is supported by insight, consciousness, conscience, integrity, tenderness, love, and courage.

The memory of the heart is more profound than the memory of the mind. Our joys and wounds stay with us much longer than memorized theorems of geometry or dates from history. This is one of the reasons why pure intellectual and social systems, no matter how logical and perfect they may be, do not change people. To change, people need a change of heart that involves a fundamental shift in perspective. Heart encompasses and integrates all the dimensions—physical, emotional, intellectual, and spiritual—of our lives. The flame of the heart has the power to move us from point A to point B, which our reason lacks. In his *Pensées*, philosopher and mathematician Blaise Pascal (1623-1662) put it nicely: "The heart has its reasons which reason does not know."

Deep in the core of our being we carry the pain of perhaps new and certainly old wounds. Our wounds are subject to infection, which can make them worse, or life and love, which can penetrate and touch and heal them. Wounds can be opportunities for wisdom and compassion. Truly effective master healers are those who also have been wounded, because they find in their own wounds, as Henri Nouwen reminds us in his book, *The Wounded Healer*, the adequate understanding, compassion, and wisdom that will help those they are helping. It is significant that the Risen Christ retained his wounds. Our wounds can become signs of hope and blessings for us and for others.

> Our wounds can become signs of hope and blessings for us and for others.

The heart, wounded or fulfilled or both, has enormous impact on our health and well-being. "Feelings," wrote surgeon and best-selling author Bernie Siegel, M.D., "are chemical and can kill or cure."

How to Get Sick

It is easy to get sick. Here are some of the ways:

- Be resentful, bitter, and critical toward others.
- Hate yourself to a degree where you completely lose self-esteem and self-respect.
- See yourself as miserable, stuck, and a failure, and don't seek any help.
- Don't identify any purpose for your life, and cultivate negative attitudes while pursuing a life without meaning or value.
- Ignore a healthy lifestyle. Don't exercise. Eat the wrong food. Drink intoxicants as much as you possible can.
- Isolate yourself. Avoid other people, especially those who are positive about life. Convince yourself that since any relationship has its own risks, it should be avoided at any cost.
- Blame others for all the problems of the world, your own problems included. Find things to complain about even when everything seems to be going well.

- Be depressed, envious, jealous, arrogant, and angry. Entertain resentment and hatred, and, when hurt, never forgive.
- Adopt a no-hope viewpoint. You will easily find this in many books, articles, TV programs, or people you somehow attract.
- Quit your job for some good reason, which you can certainly find, and become addicted to TV. Choose especially the TV shows that are boring and destructive of life and values.
- Don't believe in God. Ignore the Commandments. Give up hope. Refuse to love.

There is no worse fate for someone than to live alone, unloving and unloved. When a person has no one to love or to be loved by, then suicide begins to seem attractive. It is a shame to see many get sick or die because they have not drunk from the healing waters of the heart.

How to Stay Well or Get Better

There are many ways to stay well or to get better. Here are some of them:

- Think and act in healthy ways.

- Choose the motto, "happy, healthy, and holy" and post it on the wall, on your refrigerator, or on your desk, and especially in your mind, heart, and soul.
- Formulate a clear purpose for your life that brings you a sense of fulfillment, worth, and joy.
- Create for yourself a positive environment, be it with the friends you want to spend time with, the books and articles you read, or the shows you watch.
- Keep a sense of humor, and let your laughter convey your inner joy.
- Picture yourself accomplishing the goals you have in mind and achieving what you really want in your life.
- Appreciate the truth and depth of Francis de Sales's words: "The soul cannot live without love," as well as the words penned by the Greek dramatist Sophocles about twenty-four hundred years ago: "One word frees us of all the weight and pain of life: that word is love."
- Love God. Believe that God is in charge. Stop worrying. Relax. Meditate. Pray. "God is able to provide you with every blessing in abundance" (2 Cor 9:11). Know that God has a plan for you: "I

know the plans I have for you, says the Lord, plans for your welfare and not for your harm, to give you a future with hope" (Jer 29:11). Do you remember that train you missed, that job you couldn't get, that opportunity you lost, that traffic jam you couldn't avoid, that meeting you desperately were looking forward to but which was canceled because of the storm? You may know later on, or you may never know until eternity, how God's love was protecting you and guiding you.

• Love others. Loving, honest, and healthy relationships allow for the expression and fulfillment of the needs of intimacy, security, and mutual growth. So long as your love flows between you and others you will live, because to live is to love and to love is to live. Healthy is the heart that beats for others.

• Choose a cause you enjoy and bring your contribution to it. This will make your community, and the world, a better place.

• Love yourself. Know yourself, accept yourself, and grow from there to your full potential. Release all negative emotions such as resentment, fear, anger, and sadness. Forgive those who caused these emotions, and forgive yourself as well. Then develop the things that make you grow at all levels. Take care of your body. Take care of your mind. Take care of your heart. Take care of your soul. The healthier and more fulfilled you are, the more love you can give to others.

What's Love Got to Do With Healing?

Most people do not reach the fullness of life that God intended for them. Somehow they remain constantly tortured by fears, guilt, doubts, rejections, addictions, and all sorts of frustrations and anxieties that lead unmistakably to physical illnesses. They resolutely fill their closets with what the world of advertising offers to them, hoping to be happy now and pay later. But their secret pain never leaves the closet of their heart because their buried emotions never recover.

Recent research in spirituality and human sciences indicates that the experience of love is essential for healing, for promoting human change and growth, and for reaching the human fulfillment that gives glory to God. "God is love" (1 Jn 4:16), and love is the healing power. Believe me, many of those who are rotting in hospitals, jails, or their own loneliness are there because they have failed to grasp the nature and significance of love and consequently have wasted their energy. Their love may have focused on lust, possessions, wealth, or some other empty object, when love was supposed to give them new life.

The experience of love is essential for healing.

God's love heals the separation between us and God, between each one of us and others, and between us and the natural world. We already know enough about psychosomatic medicine to conclude that human illnesses have many dimensions—spiritual, emotional, mental, and physical—and that love is an important element in healing many of these illnesses. Illnesses that respond to love include heart problems, infections, cancer, inflammations, injuries, and depression, as well as emotional distresses such as old hurts and wounds, abuse, fears, anger, shame, grief, and despair.

Modern psychology knows that an infant can die or suffer serious retardation in growth and development from lack of love. Lack of love predisposes the infant to a hopeless/helpless attitude, which is the unmistakable prescription for all kinds of mental and physical diseases later in life. Poison is not only chemical. Poison can be spiritual, social, and emotional. Poison kills regardless of its origin.

> Love and peace help us to overcome the problems of life.

By contrast, an infant surrounded by love and peace will grow faster and will have a stronger immune function. Love and peace help us to overcome the problems of life, protect us, and teach us to survive. Bernie Siegel, M.D., put it clearly:

> As a surgeon I have worked for many years with patients suffering from life-threatening and debilitating diseases. In the course of this work, I have discovered that if such people can be brought to love themselves, some incredibly wonderful things begin to happen to them, not only psychologically but also physically. The by-product of their improved psychological attitude is a corresponding physical improvement. So, for me, the most important focus of therapy is that of teaching people how to feel and express love. And this, I have found, depends on my ability to love them and show them they are lovable.

Psychiatrist and best-selling author Gerald Jampolsky, M.D., is equally emphatic when he writes: "Healing is knowing that the only reality in the universe is love, and that love is the most important healer known to the world." He also wrote: "For me, the healing process is made up of unconditional love, forgiveness, and letting go of fear. It is that simple."

Gary Schwartz, Ph.D., and Linda Russek, Ph.D., researchers at the University of Arizona, conducted a study of college students and found that having been loved as a child has a direct correlation with good health later in life. Also they found that eighty-seven percent of those who were not loved had a chronic physical illness.

Dean Ornish, M.D., clinical professor of medicine at the University of California, San Francisco, writes: "When you feel loved, nurtured, cared for, supported and intimate, you are much more likely to be happier and healthier. You have a much lower risk of getting sick and, if you do, a much greater chance of surviving." He also affirmed, "Love and intimacy are at the root of what makes us sick and what makes us well, what causes sadness and what brings happiness, what makes us suffer and what leads to healing."

Albert Einstein said: "Many times a day I realize how much my own outer and inner life is built upon the labor of my fellow men, both living and dead, and how earnestly I must exert myself in order to give in return as much as I have received." He also said: "Only a life lived for others is worth living."

A life lived and given for others is called altruism—another name for love. Scientists now acknowledge that doing good for others is good for the doers because a genuine altruism may give their immune systems a boost.

A study was conducted on students at Harvard who were asked to watch three films: one on gardening, one a Nazi war documentary, and one on Mother Teresa, who dedicated her life and charitable works to the poor, the lepers, the orphans, and the dying. Not surprisingly, those who watched the film on Mother Teresa showed a significant increase in protective antibodies—a physical change that could possibly help them stay healthy and become healthier by improving their immune function.

Volunteering, caring for, and helping others is healthful not only for those who are helped, but also for those who perform these good deeds. Everyone, especially elderly people, likes to feel needed. Services to the community give a certain meaning to life so that one is encouraged to keep going on. Doctors agree on the importance and the benefits of volunteer work with the elderly. They have noticed that these elderly people will visit the doctors less often and complain much less. People who find meaning in helping others give meaning to their own lives. In the process, they may discover new talents and abilities they were not aware of. Paradoxically, when they lose themselves, they will find their true selves and liberate themselves from a painful existential malaise.

People who find meaning in helping others give meaning to their own lives.

Harvard cardiologist Herbert Benson, well-known for his research on the effects of relaxation, suggests that helping others can have the same effects found in yoga, spirituality, and meditation. It helps the caregiver to "forget oneself, to experience decreased metabolic rates and blood pressure, heart rate, and other health benefits."

Yale University professor of public health Lowell Levin says: "When you're a helper, your self-concept improves. You are somebody. You are worthwhile. And there's nothing more exhilarating than that. That can influence your health." But why does this contact with other people have such an influence on health?

Robert Ornstein, Ph.D., and David Sobel, M.D., in

their book, *The Healing Brain*, offer the following explanation. They say that the brain's major function is to protect the body from illness rather than to generate logical thinking. Therefore, the brain

> cannot do its job of protecting the body without contact with other people. It draws vital nourishment from our friends, lovers, relatives, lodge brothers and sisters, even perhaps our co-workers and members of our weekly bowling team....People need people. Not only for the practical benefits which derive from group life, but for our very health and survival. Somehow interaction with the larger social world of others draws our attention outside of ourselves, enlarges our focus, enhances our ability to cope, and seems to make the brain reactions more stable and the person less vulnerable to disease.

Creativity is the highest expression of love.

There is also another aspect of love that we sometimes tend to forget. Love is creative. It is true that loving brings fulfillment to a true lover, but it is also true that to be loved has the power to transform the beloved into a new person. Love can create a new self that cannot be accomplished in other ways. Creativity is the highest expression of love. A loving support between parents and children, wives and husbands, priests and parishioners, and among friends has the power to create new persons.

That new person can be and is, in reality, the person God wants us to be, the person without which we can never be happy or healed. When illness results from deviating from the path of living our true purpose in life, it takes a loving voice to tell us, "You're not being the best person you can be," to effect an immediate improvement. We have to keep in mind that if a toxic social environment can cause diseases, a loving support system can heal them. The microbiologist Louis Pasteur (1822-1895) is reported to have said on his deathbed: "Le germe n'est rien, c'est le terrain qui est tout" (The microbe is nothing, the soil is everything).

Also, love has the power to heal because it "casts out fear" (1 Jn 4:18). The real opposition is not between love and hate, but between love and fear. Fear paralyzes us. When we are not afraid, our whole self—body, mind, heart, and soul—has a great sense of well-being. We function more effectively at all levels. If fear sickens, destroys, and paralyzes, love reconciles, integrates, and provides hope and courage to move on. It helps us relax and gives us wings in search of the healing Truth.

Love extends its healing power to pets. In many cases, pets are considered part of the family. Many studies have shown that animals handled without love have weakened immune systems, and people exposed to loving animals are better able to resist disease and have a higher rate of recovery from sickness. Delta Society, a leading international organization, is known for its dedication to promoting the power of animals for people's health and well-being. The common conviction in this organization is that people who own pets have lower blood pressure, triglycerides, and cholesterol. They feel less lonely and isolated. They go to the doctor less frequently than those who do not own pets. Their mental health is better. They cope better with everyday stress.

Pets also have positive effects on children. Best-selling author Leo Buscaglia, Ph.D., was right to affirm: "If raising and caring for pets helps us learn how to be more loving and caring friends, lovers, parents, etc., then we are fortunate in having them. If they put us more in touch with all living things and our responsibilities to tend to them carefully and lovingly, then we can indeed be thankful that trillions of them are around."

It is fair to say that if most of our problems are related to the lack of love, the way of healing must be the way of love. By bringing us closer to God and others, love will heal us, renew us, and help us find our true identity in communion with God through communion with one another. "No one has ever seen God; if we love one another, God lives in us, and his love is perfected in us" (1 Jn 4:12).

Indeed, love makes us healthy, happy, and holy. It transforms us. It opens the door to the divine. It makes our life a song and brings us great grace. Love is the only sanity there is—sanity whose harmony should shape human life at its core.

FOR YOUR REFLECTION AND RESPONSE

1. How connected are you to your heart? Do you allow God and others into your feelings? Are your feelings like a passing cloud, or do they run deep in your heart and soul? Does it scare you to feel deeply? Does your mind control your feelings? Are you afraid to love? Are you afraid to be loved? Have you been hurt many times? What did you do to heal?

2. What do you think is the difference between loving yourself and selfishness? Is loving yourself good, bad, or neutral? Can you hate and hurt yourself? Do you really love yourself? If not, what are the fears and obstacles that stand in the way of your doing so? What makes you be yourself?

3. What made Jesus the greatest teacher of love? What does Jesus' revelation about God's indwelling mean to you? Is it difficult for you to think of God as a loving Father and a caring friend? Who is your neighbor? Can you name your friends and your enemies? Do you agree with Martin Luther King, Jr., who said: "Love is the only force capable of transforming an enemy into a friend"?

4. Do you feel jealous? Do you harbor resentment against anyone, yourself included? Do you hate someone? Is there anyone in your life you don't want to forgive? What is the main difficulty you see in your character which makes you sometimes do things in a non-loving manner? Do you still nurse old wounds, anger, or feelings of bitterness that poison your heart? What are the greatest obstacles to self-acceptance and to the acceptance of others?

5. Imagine yourself in the company of Jesus at the time he commanded his disciples to love one another, and imagine yourself asking him to help you overcome your dysfunctional tendencies, and to "be made well" (Jn 5:6). How do you feel if he says to you, "You are healed. Take up your life and go in peace and love"? In the midst of a crisis, what makes you feel protected? Name some ways you refuse to depend on God.

6. Have you known anyone who recovered from a grave illness? Did a loving presence make any difference in his or her recovery? Does a close relationship with God mean that a cure is certain or that we no longer need other people?

Repeat this several times a day

God's love flows through me, to each and every one I meet.

PRAYER

Dear God, I want you to be with me always, in the very center of my life. Help me open the windows of my mind and unlock the doors of my heart, so that I can reach my neighbor and love my enemy.

Make me always remember that your good news is love and that healing is based on this good news. Guide my path to a lonely heart and suffering soul and body so you can touch them through me, your instrument. Let my life bring a little more light where days are night. Let others see the face of Christ in me, and let me see the face of Christ in others.

Move my heart to always thank you for those you gave me to love. Teach us to love one another and, by doing so, heal each other. Amen.

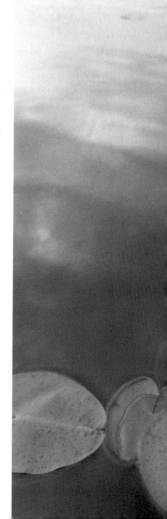

Philosopher and mathematician René Descartes (1596-1650) did not have it exactly right when he concluded, "I think, therefore I am."

Not to depreciate the value of rational thought, but it is naïve to believe that human beings live only by intellectual systems, fantastic ideas, and great ideals. Life does not take place in the lecture hall. This is one of the reasons why some of our institutions are losing their attraction. Psychiatrist Otto Rank (1884-1939) once said, "The only therapy is life." Isn't this true?

Life is love. This is what God is. Love is the experience of God. Love is our essence. All the roads of love will lead eventually to

Every relationship should be ultimately a relationship with God.

Love. Even if one starts by unknowingly taking a wrong direction, sooner or later those with pure hearts will discover the true path. They will find that God, the source of love, is at the end of the road. The love that is real and true is the love of God, and it remains constant.

Every relationship should be ultimately a relationship with God, because God is supposed to be the very ground of our being. Love, taken seriously, is a threat to the world, because it is revolutionary and it turns the world on its head.

John of the Cross believed that at the end of our lives we won't be judged by our achievements and successes, but by love; not by what we accomplished, but by how much we loved. "In the evening of life," he said, "we will be judged on love alone."

Love embraces the entire being. When one loves, one does not love just intellectually. Love uses the integrated soul-heart-mind-body entity. Who and what we love or do not love reveal our entire story. Our love is our very existence. Descartes should rather have said, "I love, therefore I am."

The most important work in life is to unlock the doors to our whole potential. It is true that locks ensure safety. But they can also make prisons. Prisons are, at least theoretically, the safest places on earth. But who wants to be there, just for the sake of safety? We want to be free, to grow, to reach our fullest potential. We want to free ourselves from old habits and blind spots. We long to develop the full range of our talents, sensitivities, and depths. We want to live to the fullest.

Love is the most fundamental need. Love makes us grow. Love dispels all fears. Love heals. Love unlocks the doors to our entire being. Loving is living and living is loving. Psychotherapist and author Viktor Frankl wrote in his famous book *Man's Search for Meaning*:

> A thought transfixed me: For the first time in my life I saw the truth as it is set into song by so many poets, proclaimed as the final wisdom by so many thinkers. The truth—that love is the ultimate and highest goal to which man can aspire. Then I grasped the meaning of the greatest secret that human poetry and human thought and belief have to impart: the salvation of man is through love and in love.

If we are able—I hope we all are one day—to fill our hearts with the eternal love that allows us to post a No Vacancy sign, we will have found the answer to loneliness and to the many problems of life. This answer is not found in any other place because ultimately everything relies on the heart—everything. We can enact the most enlightened laws, create the best systems, and discuss the best theories; nothing is going to change if there is no change of heart. Love first and then do all these things.

Augustine gave us this famous line: *Ama et fac quod vis* (Love and do what you will). Why? Because it is through our true love that grace flows through the channels of our heart and brain, and directs us to do the right thing. It is difficult to embrace this revolution of the heart, but it is not impossible. God loves to help us do even impossible things (see Mt 19:26; Mk 10:27; Lk 18:27).

Brother Laurence, in *The Practice of the Presence of God*, summarized it this way: "All things are possible to him who believes; still more to him who hopes; still more to him who loves; and most of all to him who practices all three."